The
PRIVATE
FINANCE
INITIATIVE

THE ESSENTIAL GUIDE

THE ROYAL
INSTITUTION
OF CHARTERED
SURVEYORS

Please note: References to the masculine include, where appropriate, the feminine.

Published by RICS Business Services Limited
a wholly owned subsidiary of
The Royal Institution of Chartered Surveyors
under the RICS Books imprint
12 Great George Street
London SW1P 3AD

ISBN 0 85406 702 7

CONTENTS

PREFACE

The Private Finance Initiative, or "PFI", is something that many people have heard about but which few really understand. Failure to grasp the significance of the PFI is rapidly becoming a major handicap to anyone involved in funding or carrying out projects for the public sector.

The PFI is not simply about funding big infrastructure projects such as bridges and motorways. Increasingly it is the means through which hospitals, schools and even prisons are built. Many public-sector bodies are now required to consider the availability of private finance before embarking on any construction project.

To help guide potential users of the PFI through the maze, the RICS, with support from the Department of the Environment, commissioned Chesterton, the international property consultants, to produce an easy-to-read guide to the Initiative.

The Guide provides answers to some key questions about the PFI:

*   How does it work?

*   Where is it relevant?

*   How is value for money assessed?

*   How are the risks shared?

*   How can you avoid some of the pitfalls?

The PFI is here to stay. This new Guide is the essential starting point for anyone wanting to find out more about the Initiative.

THE PRIVATE FINANCE INITIATIVE - WHAT IS IT?

The Private Finance Initiative (PFI) is the name given to the policies announced by the Chancellor of the Exchequer in the Autumn Statement of 1992. His intention was to bring the private sector into the provision of services and infrastructure which, formerly, have always been regarded as primarily "Public". The changes involved relaxation in the rules governing financially free-standing projects; the encouragement of joint ventures between public and private sectors; and an undertaking that the government would look for further opportunities for the private sector to provide capital intensive services to the public sector.

The aim of the PFI is to increase the flow of capital projects against a background of restraint on public expenditure. The public sector is encouraged to bring the private-sector more centrally into the operation of capital assets. It is aimed at harnessing private sector management skills, and at a transfer of risk away from the public sector, onto the private sector.

The Treasury have said from the outset that there is to be no fixed or rigid definition of a PFI project - the PFI depends not on rules, but on a set of principles which are being applied in different ways in different parts of the public sector according to their needs.

Although announced some time ago, it is hard to exaggerate the importance of the PFI, the impact which it will have on the construction industry, and on all those who provide services of any kind to the public sector.

IS IT A SUCH A NEW IDEA?

The PFI is only the latest, even if arguably the most sophisticated, in a series of measures designed to reform public service provision in the UK.

The role of the government is to make policy, not to provide services

Since 1979 the government has sought to involve the private sector in ever wider areas of the economy in the belief that private sector enterprise and disciplines can bring gains in efficiency and reductions in cost. The public sector should aim wherever possible, not at providing services itself, but at purchasing services from the private sector, and enabling the private sector to provide them.

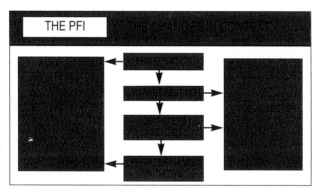

Privatisation was designed to take certain services entirely outside the public sector - services which could reasonably be regarded as having nothing to do with government. In a privatised service the private sector takes complete control, subject only to a system of regulation laid down by statute, and assumes all of the risk.

A further batch of initiatives, including the Next Steps Agencies and the introduction of Market Testing, followed now by the PFI, are aimed at public services, and are intended to transfer the responsibility for their delivery away from the public, to the private sector. But in the Next Steps Agencies - of which there are now 108 - and in the Market Testing Initiative, both control and risk, stay in the public sector.

The PFI is different. Control, together with the greater part of the risk, is intended to pass to the private sector. In this sense, the

PFI resembles the privatisation initiative. The principle underpinning all these reforms is that although the government may need to be responsible for the delivery of a particular service, or with the capital expenditure associated with providing it, the government does not necessarily have to be responsible for managing the service, or for undertaking the investment itself.

WHY DO YOU NEED TO KNOW ABOUT PRIVATE FINANCE INITIATIVE?

Because the PFI is mandatory. If an organisation wants to get involved with supplying central government, the consideration of the private finance option is mandatory. Government departments and all public sector bodies directly sponsored by them have to consider private finance before embarking on traditional procurement routes. Local Authorities are being encouraged to follow. Measures to increase the incentives for them to use PFI principles throughout their fields of activity were introduced in April 1995. More changes can be expected to follow.

Where the use of private finance in the central government sector can deliver better value for money than the publicly funded alternative, and the private sector assumes genuine risk, approval for traditional methods of procurement will not be given.

It follows that all central government proposals which involve capital expenditure, and many which involve revenue expenditure, have to be examined to determine which route is likely to maximise value for money and risk transfer.

THE THEORY

A high proportion of PFI schemes will involve the development of land and buildings as a secondary output, but it is vital to remember that the PFI is not directly concerned with the provision of buildings.

The only reason why governments or Local Authorities occupy buildings, or use public money to assist in their provision, is to help them deliver services or achieve policy objectives. However, one does not need to own a building to obtain a service delivered from it, or even to take all the risks involved in running the service. The fact that the service is delivered efficiently and at least cost is what matters to government.

The point can be explained by analogy. If a private individual wants, say, legal advice, he simply contacts a solicitor. He does not dream of building or leasing an office and employing his own solicitors. He purchases the service, and the provider of the service is responsible for the premises he works from, and everything else connected with giving his client good value for money. A solicitor's fees include an element for rent, rates and occupation costs of his office. The solicitor takes the risk, both on these elements of cost, and on the likelihood of the client wanting further service from him.

The government is seeking to extend this principle to the services which it needs.

The point to grasp is that there are no public benefits arising from the ownership or provision of buildings as such: the benefits arise from the purpose for which they are used. Furthermore:

• the occupation of buildings, whether owned or occupied, carries with it certain risks which have nothing to do with the service being delivered;

• the management and maintenance of a building over its lifetime is greatly influenced by its original design and specification. Increased efficiency in the management of the facility can (a) justify an alternative approach to design, and (b) provide a means for capturing long-term savings and a reduction in risk.

If one compares the initial cost of a building with the net present cost of operating it over, say 20 or 25 years, the initial costs are extremely small. The PFI seeks to reflect this, and to restore a better balance to capital expenditure appraisal, by placing the responsibility for long-term management within the same contract as the initial design .

The transfer of risk from the public to the private sector, improvements in efficiency and reductions in the aggregate cost of providing a service over time are the principles on which the PFI is founded.

HOW DOES IT WORK?

The "Purchaser" and the "Operator"

The structure of projects differs widely. Sometimes the purchaser for the service being provided is not the public, but the public sector itself - as in the health service. Sometimes the output required is not a service at all in the conventional sense.

PFI schemes which depend on the delivery of a service have come to be known as "classic" PFI. This distinguishes them from economic development and regeneration schemes where the government is buying, not a service, but a policy objective - a different kind of aim, but equally susceptible to a PFI approach. The principles are the same, but the appropriate structures are different.

In "classic" PFI there are just two parties to an agreement: the public sector client, referred to throughout the rest of this Guide as The Purchaser; and the private sector supplier, referred to from now on as The Operator. In the field of economic development and regeneration, the term "developer" might be substituted for Operator.

The Purchaser agrees a long-term service contract with the Operator. The contract must demonstrate value for money to the Purchaser, and the Operator must assume risk - the degree of risk varying according to the nature of the deal.

Value for money and adequate risk transfer are imperatives: the PFI does not necessarily replace traditional ways in which the public sector delivers services, or even the way it procures buildings. Value for money and risk transfer must first be proven, and if they are not, traditional methods remain in place.

Where justified, a new kind of relationship

Nonetheless, where value for money and risk transfer can be demonstrated, and the Purchaser seeks to use private finance, the PFI route is fundamentally incompatible with traditional fragmented procurement devices, like public sector building contracts, or full repairing and insuring leases to public sector occupiers.

Though advisers may be required to guide purchasers through the PFI process, the traditional construction team - architects, surveyors, engineers, project managers - work for the private sector Operator of the service, not for the public sector Purchaser.

WHERE IS THE PFI RELEVANT?

Right Across the Public Sector

The PFI is relevant wherever the public sector seeks to achieve objectives of any kind which involve buildings or any other form of capital expenditure.

Usually, these objectives call for the delivery of some service or other from the building - healthcare, for example, education, or some kind of social service. This is "classic" PFI as has been described.

Occasionally, the building serves some other purpose, such as the provision of employment, affordable housing, or other bene-fits to the community. This is a slightly different, and much longer established area in which private and public sectors share risk to achieve their different objectives, but the thinking behind it stands four-square with the PFI.

This type of activity is sponsored in England and Northern Ireland by the Department of the Environment, and by the Scottish and Welsh Offices in Scotland and Wales. It is often conducted through agencies, like English Partnerships, the Scottish Enterprise Network or the Welsh Development Agency.

Classic PFI: Acquiring Services

Typically, this core area works as follows. The government itself through a department of state like the Home Office, or a public body sponsored by a department, like a Health Trust, wishes to expand or modify the service it gives. This body becomes the Purchaser. The project is known to involve substantial capital investment, but what the Purchaser seeks to buy is not the building, but the service conducted from it - whether it be a prison, or a new hospital.

The prime interest of the Purchaser lies, therefore, in finding a reliable and efficient Operator of the facility. The Operator is expected to procure the necessary buildings himself, and to charge the public sector customer for the service. The cost of the service will include an element for amortisation of the capital expenditure, as well as elements covering the revenue costs, profit, risk, etc.

Often the Operator will be in consortium with a contractor, but there is no reason why this should be so, other than to capture the design-and-build skills, and financial muscle, which such a partner can contribute. A service operator with a sufficiently strong covenant could equally well lead a PFI bid.

PFI is particularly suitable for services which are heavily dependent on capital expenditure. In fact, the only practical limit to the scope of the PFI is what is politically acceptable.

Just as there is no theoretical limit to the range of services which can be provided, so it is also possible to split the responsibility for the service. In most cases for the time being however, the private sector will supply a building, heat it, light it and maintain it, whilst the public sector provides the education, the healthcare or the social service which goes on inside it.

PFI in Housing, Economic Development and the Environment

The PFI gives a boost to the development of public/private joint ventures and partnerships in this field. In England, Northern Ireland, Wales and Scotland, grant assistance awarded on very similar principles have been in operation since 1983. However, in recent years there has been a tendency to move away from grants into more flexible longer term arrangements, including joint ventures and the PFI provides a clearer framework within which this use of private finance can be explored further.

There are four principal channels through which the government hopes to achieve policy objectives using the PFI in England:

• through Local Authorities, recently freed by changes in their ability to go into joint ventures with the private sector. Further changes are likely;

- by means of agencies, of which English Partnerships is much the most important. The English Partnerships *Investment Guide* is deliberately based on PFI principles;

- by means of the Single Regeneration Budget, an agglomeration of various different sources of cash for regeneration, administered by the DOE through new government offices for the regions;

- using the "Local Investment Fund" (LIF), a public/private joint venture between the corporate and voluntary sectors, aimed at helping voluntary organisations to contribute to urban regeneration.

In Wales, changes similar to those in England have been introduced to encourage the use of PFI in the local government sector. In Scotland, the Scottish Enterprise national network of Local Enterprise Companies have for some time been operating PFI principles.Throughout the United Kingdom, there is a change of attitude and approach which is leading to a harmonisation and clearer definition of the government's value for money objectives in the environment . All this can be traced back to the PFI.

WHAT DO YOU HAVE TO PROVE?

There are two imperatives in the PFI, each of them closely related to the other, but best dealt with separately in presentation and analysis.

1. Value for Money

Private money costs more

Private money is more expensive than public money. In strictly financial terms, where there is no difference in the cost of management or in the efficiency with which the building can be used, it will always cost less if a project is carried out using public, rather than private, money. The provision of private finance by private promoters does not itself bring economic benefits. The involvement of the private sector in public projects can only be justified when it represents good value for money.

But what is the alternative?

Is it always the one which is 100% funded with public money? Not in all cases. There is no need to compare a proposal with a publicly funded alternative where:

• there is no public money needed, i.e. the project is financially free-standing and returns are adequate to cover private sector risk without any financial input from government; and

• there is no public money available, and no realistic prospect that a scheme could go ahead on a similar timescale.

Neither of these exclusions removes the need for the public sector to be satisfied that the proposal before them is the most cost-effective which could reasonably be achieved using private finance. This objective is usually satisfied by means of competition.

Where the project needs some form of public sector investment, and where there is a realistic prospect of using public money, rather than private money, it is necessary to compare the part-privately financed route with the publicly financed one. This test, known as the value for money test, is designed to show that the government contribution is not at the expense of other, better, uses for the money.

The test applies only to the government (or public sector) contribution to the project.

The test is carried out as follows:

(a) Value the costs and benefits

Essentially, this is a matter of measuring the additional cost of private finance and establishing that its use is justified by the public sector benefits it brings with it. Benefits which are common to both methods of financing must, of course, be excluded. The marginal cost of using private finance is compared with the marginal value to the public sector. Where the value exceeds the cost, value for money is established.

(b) Use the Green Book

Techniques for testing value for money are set out in the Treasury's *"Green Book", Economic Appraisal in Central Government - A technical guide for Government Departments.* It is available through HMSO, and is widely used as a "bible" by practitioners in both public and private sectors. Anyone involved with trying to make PFI work is strongly advised to consult it.

(c) Appraise the options

Appraisal in the public sector is founded on the consideration of the available options, and the identification of costs, benefits and uncertainties associated with each one. It is important not to forget the "do nothing" option.

(d) Discount to present value

Discounted Cash Flow techniques, as recommended in the *Green Book,* are used as a means of putting each of these on a comparable basis, reducing each to a Net Present Value (NPV). Due allowance needs to be made for economic displacement in valuing benefits, and all sunk costs must be ignored. It is normal practice to express everything in real terms, i.e. at a general, specified price level without allowance for inflation.

(e) Choose the appropriate discount rate

In most cases involving central government, the discount rate to be used is 6%. Exceptions include industrial and economic development proposals (whether for grants or for PFI-type joint ventures) where the discount rate is set at 8%.

(f) Evaluate intangible costs and benefits

Some benefits, and some costs, cannot be valued in money terms. These include risk transfer, qualitative improvements in service, improvements to the environment and other social or intangible outputs. These so-called "non-marketed" outputs must nonetheless be considered and evaluated. Methodologies for doing this usually depend on some method of "scoring" the outputs against an appropriate scale.

(g) Choose the winner

The best option is the one which shows the highest Net Present Value, after crediting the benefits with non-marketed outputs.

(h) Present the results

Skillful presentation of a cost benefit analysis is extremely important. In simple terms, the NPV of the scheme is the measure of the cost to the public sector of adopting the private option. Although the numbers are important, the intangible element is significant in many PFI schemes. Whilst many of these cannot be valued or costed, rigorous appraisal of them counts for a great deal, particularly in the environment field.

Remember, however, that demonstration of value for money is not enough, on its own, to validate a PFI deal: it is also necessary to show that risk has been transferred from the public to the private sector.

2. Risk Transfer

The transfer of risk onto the private sector, and away from the public sector, is one of the benefits associated with the use of private finance, and, as such, has to be considered in value for money analysis as outlined above. However, in PFI, risk transfer has to be considered in some senses as an end in itself, and must as such be evaluated independently of value for money appraisal, even if subsequently wrapped up in an over-all value for money judgement.

Some risks are easily transferred

At one level, risk transfer is clearly and easily achieved. Some risks are normal features of contracts for the provision of services and associated capital expenditure in the private sector.

The private sector should expect to bear all of the risk in the following areas in PFI contracts:

* design
* construction, both as to quality and cost
* maintenance

- operation of the service contract and facilities management
- finance.

These are normal private sector risks.

Others may stay with the public sector

"Systematic" or "procedural" risks, are outside the influence of the Operator, and have to remain with the public sector. They include such things as changes in government policy, the chance that planning permission will be refused, or that the Purchaser might be acting outside its powers

But trading risks should be shared

The term trading risks actually includes two types of risk - volume risk (will the demand for the service reach the levels predicted?) and pricing (will the Purchaser be able to afford the price quoted?).

Where PFI principles are used to fulfil policy objectives, rather than provide services, this is not an issue: the private sector is used to taking the risks involved in constructing buildings and finding occupiers in fields like housing and economic development.

In the core area of "classic" PFI, where the objective is to buy services, however, things are not so simple. The authorities insist that the PFI is not to be used as borrowing by another name. A guaranteed income stream from a public sector purchaser over a number of years, irrespective of demand for the service, is regarded as insulating the private sector against the vagaries of the Purchaser's market-place and therefore fails to meet one of the central objectives of the PFI.

Many public sector Purchasers are themselves in a market place. There is some pressure, therefore, for the Operator of the service to identify himself with the risks faced by the Purchaser, and to take some share of them, both as to volume and price.

Examples arise in the Health Sector, where the workings of the internal market mean that a Health Trust will not be able to guarantee usage. Similarly, the Home Office cannot guarantee take up of its planned Secure Training Centres. Other PFI schemes likely to come forward depend at least partly for their viability on revenue from the paying public, and demand may go up or down.

Wherever the service is wholly or partly influenced by market demand, it is more or less inevitable that the private sector operator will be required to share in that aspect of the risk.

There are no rules concerning risk transfer. The PFI is, as the present Chancellor has said, deal driven in this respect, not rule-driven.

AVOIDING THE PITFALLS

Competition

The dream

It has been a public sector dream for many years that all the government needed to do to was to find a way of "unlocking" private sector creativity, and harnessing this quality for the public good. Some of the publicity surrounding the launch of the PFI was aimed in this direction. According to this scenario, the PFI makes it possible to approach government and take the initiative in proposing almost anything which involves the provision of a public sector service, or a way to discharge government policy - together, of course, with related building works.

The guidance

The Treasury published guidance for government departments in March 1994 (*Competition and the Private Finance Initiative*) setting out its stall in this area, but repeating its belief in the idea of competition. However, it accepts that in exceptional circumstances there may be a case for alternatives to competitive tendering, in the interests of stimulating innovation.

Subject to EC rules, departments may deal with a single promoter, where the promoter:

* identifies an entirely new project;

* responds to an invitation from a public sector body, where the outputs are not specifically defined but come within broad functions, policies or initiatives;

- proposes a solution to a project already identified by the public sector which has a genuinely innovative element.

The best way of making competition more attractive to the private sector, says the relevant guidance note, is by "focusing the competitive process more sharply". Specifications should be based on final outputs, which leave a contractor the opportunity to offer ideas. There should be a clear and precise statement of the rights, obligations and responsibilities of each of the parties and clear evaluation criteria. The guidance note argues that the fewer the number of variables subject to competition, the better.

Specific suggestions include tendering at the earliest possible stage in the process for all subsequent stages; establishing a definite timescale and limiting bidders invited to submit tenders to no more than three or four. In certain circumstances, departments are advised that they may consider announcing in advance arrangements for contributing to the costs incurred by a limited number of pre-qualified bidders, where they consider that this might enhance the quality of the competition.

The reality

Circumstances will obviously vary, but it is clear that benefits of competition continue to be highly valued in public sector procurement. Single tender dealing will continue to be the exception rather than the rule. Private sector Operators, including those who are essentially property developers, will continue to have to come up with something a great deal more than a good idea if they wish to avoid the idea being put out to competition.

An important consequence of this is that the role of the public sector in initiating PFI schemes, working them up to the stage when bids can be invited, and subsequently evaluating proposals is much enhanced. This matter is dealt with in greater detail below.

Specification by Outputs

The dream

One of the most attractive features of the PFI is the requirement to specify the service required, i.e. the output - rather than the means of supplying it (the input). The idea is to leave the bidder with the greatest possible amount of freedom to come up with innovative solutions.

The reality

In fact, specification by outputs is not a simple matter. Tendering is expensive for Operators, and if Purchasers do not articulate their requirements exactly and completely, the uncertainty created translates itself into an additional cost. Tendering risks become too great, and the competitive process falls apart.

In "classic" PFI cases, where the public sector objective is to acquire services, the problem is caused by the perception - shared equally by Purchaser and prospective Operators - that the Purchaser's own staff must be content with the operational capacity of the facility provided if the bid is to have any chance of success. Operators need to know what those standards are, and often this requires rather more specification than might appear obvious to non-specialists in the field being covered.

In simple, non "classic" PFI cases, where the objective is to promote policy aims on particular sites, the problem is slightly different. Here the additional costs arise, not from uncertainty about what is required, but from ever greater demands for accountability, and the complexity of partnership arrangements under the Single Regeneration Budget, City Challenge Partnerships and so on.

All projects which involve building works are constrained by the need for planning consent. Failure to incorporate the planning framework within the specification will, at the very least, introduce delay and uncertainty into the bidding process. At worst, it will reduce competition, or cause an otherwise attractive bid to fail.

PFI is not a short-cut

In most cases, Purchasers will need to proceed much as they would have to if they were commissioning a design-and-build solution. Added to this is the need to specify the service required from an Operator, especially at the interface between Operator's and Purchaser's personnel.

This has important consequences. For the Purchaser, these involve the time taken to launch a project and the expense of hiring specialist advice - which must now include financial and legal services, as well as PFI expertise, and the remainder of the normal buildings procurement team. There are also implications for existing staff in many cases.

There are also value for money and risk transfer implications. The more complex the service required by the Purchaser, the further the simple aim of specifying outputs is compromised by the need to reach back into the know-how and technology of the supporting capital investment. On the other hand, the greater the responsibility the public sector assumes for the definition of the buildings associated with the services, the harder it is to maximise the benefits of risk transfer.

The evidence is that a light specification simply transfers the cost of filling in the details on to the tenderer, escalates the risks in tendering and reduces private sector interest.

The best course for both public and private sectors is to maximise pre-tendering effort. The time is well spent and the costs will be recouped in the form of greater private sector interest and a keener appreciation all round about what is wanted.

Transfer of Obligations (Protection of Employment) Regulations - TUPE

Many PFI opportunities involve the effective privatisation of an existing service. The opportunity to make savings, or achieve efficiencies in comparison with what is happening at the moment, is often central to the Purchaser's objectives. In consequence, the jobs of existing public sector employees are frequently affected.

The requirement for the public sector Purchaser to compensate existing employees made redundant following contracting-out of the service can be extremely expensive. However, wherever this problem arises, it is really no more than a cost of going down the PFI route. It has to be built into the value for money appraisal, to the obvious benefit of the "do-nothing" option, or possibly the entirely publicly financed route.

The existence of this roadblock emphasises again the importance to purchasers and bidders alike of focusing on the operator aspect of PFI, not on the provision of the capital investment. The only way of absorbing the cost of TUPE is to be able to offer existing public sector employees the same terms and conditions in private employment as they enjoyed in the public sector. This calls for proposals to be backed by private sector Operators of financial standing and experience in this specialist field.

Length of the Service Contract

More accurately, this problem can be described as a difference between the length of service term which a Purchaser may wish to offer, compared to the length of term which an Operator may wish to undertake.

Many Purchasers are minded to offer the shortest possible term. This gives them more flexibility, and allows them - in theory - to consider proving value for money as often as possible by offering the service on the open market at shorter intervals, with all that this entails for the Operator's investment in the structure. Other Purchasers accept that a longer term contract will give them a lower theoretical cost, because the burden of amortising the capital (i.e. setting aside a sufficient amount from income so that it will accumulate and repay the original investment) will be lower.

Operators are motivated towards negotiating the length of term which is easiest for them to finance. Shorter periods are very expensive, and longer periods hard to finance because of incompatibility with banking practice.

The outcome depends on negotiation. In theory it ought to be possible for Purchaser and Operator to agree on shorter periods, on the basis that if the Purchaser wanted to make a change, it would be in both parties' interests that any unamortised balance of capital expenditure at the end of a shorter term should be "bundled" with a new service contract and re-tendered. The original Operator might not be pleased that he had lost the service contract, but at least he would be paid for the asset.

Generally, there is little to be said for short service contracts, because the advantages which a short-term offers to a Purchaser can be achieved in other ways.

Unamortised Balances

Having said this, the risk of coming to the end of a service contract whilst still having the remainder of the original expenditure to amortise, weighs very heavily with the private sector. It is rather like the compulsory retirement for an individual who has a large mortgage to pay off. The income stream stops (unless a new service contract is won) but the expenditure continues.

Yet PFI principles make it virtually inevitable that successful proposals involve an Operator in having an unamortised balance of capital expenditure at the end of a service contract.

The value for money factor

The greater the capital expenditure associated with the service, the greater the burden of capital charges, and the greater the threat to value for money, compared with the publicly funded alternative. Whilst the PFI route envisages capital being amortised over 15-18 years, the publicly funded alternative with which it might have to be compared would amortise the investment over 50 years. This gives the publicly funded route a huge cost advantage which may become difficult to balance with the other benefits of a PFI-type contract.

The effect of Accounting Standards for Leases and Hire Purchase Contracts

Application of relevant Accounting Standards to a service contract which lasts for the same period as it takes to amortise the building would classify it as a finance lease outside the exceptions for such leases outlined in HM Treasury Public Expenditure Survey *Private Finance: Leasing Guidance* dated 26th May 1993. The capital value of the lease would count in full against the expenditure provision of the Purchaser, and would remove from him the ability to carry the commitment "off balance sheet".

Good Practice in Value for Money Appraisal

It is stretching the imagination too much to say that a structure has a nil value at the end of a 15-year service contract. Good practice requires that a residual value is incorporated into the NPV calculation. There are two different approaches, each adopted and accepted by different government departments at present:

1. a straight 75% of today's open market value, deferred for the period - say 25 years - at the investment rate; or

2. land and buildings are separated. Land is valued at today's figure, deferred for the period, at an appropriate rate. The building element is also valued on the same basis, but the figure inserted as residual value is depreciated by an amount equal to the sum of annual straight line depreciation charges, assuming the building had a 60-year life.

Different proposals will lead to different ways of resolving these conflicts. However, one approach likely to feature strongly in successful PFI projects is the transfer of ownership.

Where award of a service contract includes an effective transfer of ownership in the relevant assets (e.g. by way of a long ground lease, or sale of the freehold or heritable interest in the land), the Operator is left in an exceptionally strong position to bid for the next service contract. It follows that he is not under such pressure to recover all his investment against the first contract, and is offered some choice about the way in which he "loads" his income stream with the burden of amortisation.

USING THE PFI

So far it has been possible to guide the newcomer through the PFI process without discriminating between the knowledge requirements of public sector Purchaser and private sector Operator. It is now helpful to look at the issues from separate ends of the telescope.

The Purchaser

Is it a PFI project at all?

To determine the answer to this question, there is very little alternative to modelling the options. The information on which this preliminary option appraisal is based need not be particularly detailed, but it will give a first reading as to whether - if there is a publicly financed alternative available or where some public sector investment is required - value for money is likely to be achieved. And it will allow a preliminary view to be formed as to whether an acceptable degree of risk transfer can be achieved.

The discipline with regard to the value for money assessment has been outlined already, and is the same at the preliminary stage even if the figures are estimates only.

With regard to risk transfer, it is useful to analyse the project with regard to the type of risks being transferred. The results can be reviewed in the light of the supply of private sector Operators capable of undertaking such risks, and the market available to them elsewhere.

As the PFI takes off, it is becoming increasingly clear that there is an acute shortage of organisations - whether operating alone or in consortium - capable of assuming the risks associated with PFI and delivering the skills required. This is probably temporary. However, it will always be necessary for would-be Purchasers to consider their output specification carefully in the light of the market into which they wish to launch it.

It is important to realise that private finance does not provide value for money in all cases. It is also perfectly possible to envisage a situation in which the PFI "works" in respect of a service in one place, but not, for the same service, in another. Location is important for private investment in land and buildings. Similarly, the "market" for the service being provided varies in quality according to location, and demographics.

The degree of specification

The first step for the Purchaser is to develop an understanding of the optimum degree of specification for the project in mind. On the one hand, he will have to take Treasury guidance into account. This proposes the minimum specification, and the minimum number of variables, with a concentration on the outputs required from an Operator.

On the other hand, the Purchaser will need to be sure that the facilities (i.e. the physical assets and structures) which the Operator proposes are fully compatible with the other, separate services - like teaching, or clinical care, or benefits distribution - which stay in the public sector, and which he will need to be able to deliver alongside the services of the Operator. This inevitably involves an interest in the design of the buildings, and the technical specification of the equipment. Although the Operator will provide these, it will be the Purchaser's staff who have to use them.

Where buildings or civil engineering work is required, Purchasers are also well advised to explore the planning situation in some detail, especially if there are listed buildings involved, or where sales of land for alternative uses are envisaged as a source of finance.

Qualification procedures

Purchasers will need to comply with EC Directives on public procurement. These are implemented in the UK under Statutory Instruments, as follows:

- Supplies Directive: SI 95/201 The Public Supply Contracts Regulations 1995

- Works Directive: SI 91/2680 The Public Works Contracts Regulations 1991

- Services Directive: SI 93/3228 The Public Services Contracts Regulations 1993

- Utilities Directive: SI 92/3279 The Utilities Supply and Works Contracts Regulations 1992.

PFI contracts will fall within the requirements of the Works Directive, the Services Directive or the Utilities Directive. The Works Directive is generally used for PFI schemes where the nature of the service cannot, at the time, be properly scoped or priced independently.

From January 1st 1996, a new Agreement on Government Procurement will replace existing texts under the auspices of the World Trade Organisation, following harmonisation of EC rules with USA. The threshold for central government supplies and services will be approximately £96,000, and for Local Authorities approximately £150,000, and for Utilities, about £300,000. The threshold for construction contracts will be about £3.75M.

Emerging practice in PFI suggests that Purchasers will generally invite initial expressions of interest by means of advertisement in the Official Journal of the European Communities, following the negotiated or the restricted procedure. A "long list" of possible Operators will then be shortened to a list of about three or four. The rejection process needs to be reasoned and structured to accord with the procurement rules.

Competitive tendering

Following pre-qualification, it is normal for the short list of chosen bidders to be invited to enter into a period of discussion with the Purchaser with a view to developing the greatest possible understanding of the project, and of the costs involved. For large projects, this period can extend for six months.

It is at this stage that the process becomes extremely costly for bidders, since they must work up their designs in some detail with no guarantee of success. In certain circumstances, where the complexity or size of the project justify it, some Purchasers elect to offer a degree of underwriting of tendering costs for selected bidders.

The Operator

The operating capability

The role of 'Operator', for service-oriented PFI, involves the requirement to combine two different kinds of businesses, that of the design-and-build contractor, and that of the provider of the service. Not only are these two businesses different in character, each of them is traditionally financed differently, measures performance differently, undertakes different kinds of risk, and attracts different kinds of investor. The British economy has not previously provided opportunities for this sort of combination, and there is a great lack of experience.

Although the construction industry contains many companies which are well equipped to fulfil the role assigned to them in PFI, and although there is a great shortage of service providers of equivalent financial muscle, there should be no doubt that in the longer term, it is the role of the service provider which is the more important.

The net present value of the income from a PFI service can be many times larger than the NPV of the building or civil engineering work involved. Without a credible service provider, the requirements of the PFI cannot be fulfilled.

Partnership

Outside the field of infrastructure, the financially free-standing project - that is, a project from which the Operator can earn a reasonable return from direct charges to the public - is likely to be extremely rare. Most PFI schemes involve a financial contribution from the public sector, and thus some form of risk sharing with the public sector. They are therefore in the nature of a partnership.

The term partnership has been much abused in connection with public/private agreements. It does not generally mean a fully equitable relationship, in which both parties share proportionately in the downside of a transaction as well as in the upside. The term joint venture is similarly abused. In all but exceptional cases, partnerships or joint ventures with the public sector contain terms limiting the public sector downside. Indeed, this is an important aspect of what the government means by risk being clearly divided.

Structures

The point to be made here is that partnerships or joint ventures with Purchasers or other public sector bodies are not always straightforward. Health Trusts, for example, are not allowed to participate in commercial companies. The powers of Local Authorities are heavily circumscribed, despite recent changes.

Outside the service-oriented sector of PFI, joint ventures and partnerships between public and private sectors can be regulated in a variety of ways, ranging from normal development agreements to limited partnerships (and even share-ownership in joint stock companies), but also including ground leases. Because this aspect of PFI is not new, a great deal of experience has been accumulated.

Where a Purchaser is acquiring services from an Operator in the newer areas of PFI, it will generally be the service agreement which regulates the partnership, with such things as the sale or ground leasing of land being covered by way of commitments to enter into parallel agreements in those areas. It may well be that other special subjects, such as the definition and regulation of operating standards, will also be hived down into separate subsidiary agreements. The supremacy of the service agreement, however, is likely to be universal.

CONCLUSION

Despite having been announced as long ago as November 1992, it is early days still for the Private Finance Initiative. This Guide is intended to assist practitioners in both public and private sectors towards an understanding of the elements of an extremely complex new order. Though based on a simple idea, the PFI reaches into so many corners of the economy that simple concepts soon give way to the need to understand the detailed problems in the area being considered

It is well said that the PFI is deal drive, not rule driven. Rules covering the whole spectrum of its applicability would be impossible to draft.

The PFI is developing very fast and it is not appropriate to attach a Bibliography to a general guide of this sort. Those wishing to be put in touch with the latest developments should contact the PFI Panel at:

35 Old Queen Street
London SW1H 9JD
Telephone: 0171 222 2866